HOW DID WE FIND OUT ABOUT
THE UNIVERSE?

HOW DID WE FIND OUT ABOUT

THE UNIVERSE?

Isaac Asimov
Illustrated by David Wool

WALKER AND COMPANY
New York

First published in the United States of America
in 1983 by the Walker Publishing Company, Inc.

This edition printed in 1985.

Published simultaneously in Canada by John Wiley & Sons Canada,
Limited, Rexdale, Ontario.

ISBN: 0-8027-6476-2 Trade
        0-8027-6477-0 Reinf.

Library of Congress Catalog Card Number: 82-42531

Printed in the United States of America

10 9 8 7 6 5 4 3 2

Dedicated to:
Millicent Selsam,
who keeps thinking up titles
—remorselessly.

Contents

1 The Stars

As far as we can see by looking at the sky, the universe is made up of the Earth and other planets, the Sun and other stars, and the Moon.

But is that all? We know there's only one Earth, one Moon, and one Sun, but what about the planets and stars? Could there be more than we see? Could there be some planets and stars that are so dim that they can't be seen even though they're there?

In 1608, a telescope was invented in Holland. Through a telescope, people could see things that were too far away or too dim to see without a telescope.

In 1609, an Italian scientist, Galileo (GA-lih-LAY-oh, 1564–1642), built a small telescope of his own and looked at the sky through it. Almost at once he found that wherever he looked in the sky, he could see many more stars with a telescope than without one.

GALILEO

In 1610, for instance, he looked at the Milky Way through the telescope. Without the telescope, the Milky Way looks like a very faint foggy belt of light that stretches across the sky. Through the telescope, however, Galileo could see that the foggy light was produced by vast crowds of very faint stars.

In that same year, Galileo looked at Jupiter and found that there were four smaller bodies that circled it. They were "satellites" (SAT-uh-lites) of Jupiter, just as the Moon is a satellite of Earth. This meant that there were more objects in the solar system, too, than could be seen just by the eye alone.

After Galileo's time, it became clear that the universe consisted not only of the solar system, but also of millions upon millions of stars.

That didn't mean that the universe had to be very large. It could be that all the stars existed in a region just beyond the solar system.

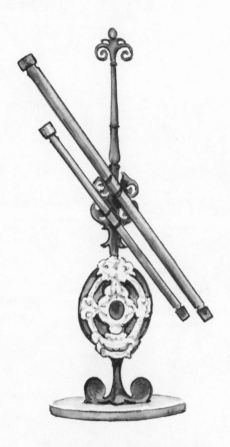

GALILEO'S TELESCOPES

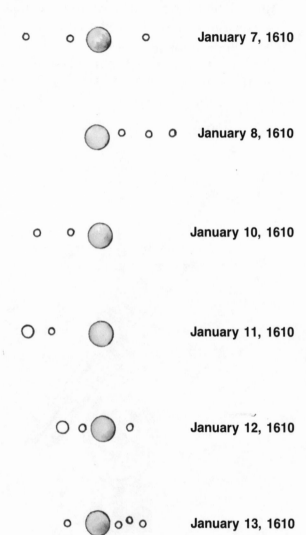

January 7, 1610

January 8, 1610

January 10, 1610

January 11, 1610

January 12, 1610

January 13, 1610

WHAT GALILEO SAW

GIOVANNI D. CASSINI

But then, how large is the solar system?

In 1671, an Italian-French astronomer, Giovanni D. Cassini (ka-SEE-nee, 1625–1712), was the first to work out how far away the planet Mars is. Once that was worked out, the distances of all the other planets of the solar system could be calculated.

Cassini's calculation was almost right. Later astronomers corrected him a little and we now know that the Sun is just about 93,000,000 miles away from the Earth. This was a lot farther than astronomers before Cassini's time had thought.

Some of the planets are even farther away from the Sun than the Earth is. The planet Saturn was the farthest known in Cassini's time and it is over 800,000,000 miles away from the Sun.

Since Cassini's time planets that are even farther away have been discovered. The farthest planet we now know, Pluto, makes an ellipse around the Sun that is over 7,000,000,000 (seven billion) miles from side to side.

Is that how big the universe is? Seven billion miles from end to end with all the stars sprinkled in a huge sphere just beyond Pluto?

A number of astronomers didn't think so. They argued that the stars were at different distances and that the dim ones were much farther away than the bright ones. They suspected that the stars were really brightly shining suns, like our own, and were no brighter than they seemed only because they were so far away. In that case, even the nearest of them would have to be much farther away than Pluto. After all, why else should they all seem so dim if they were really bright suns?

Was there any way of showing that this was actually so, or would astronomers have to guess forever?

As early as 130 B.C. Greek astronomers had found a way of measuring the distance of something in the sky. It is called "parallax" (PA-ruh-laks). To make use of

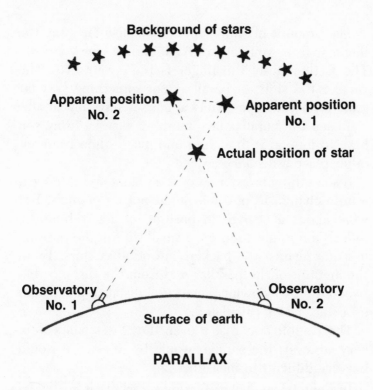

PARALLAX

parallax you must look at an object from two different places and note the way the object seems to change position.

You can see how this works if you hold your finger in front of your face, close your left eye, and look at your finger with your right eye. You will see that it is near a particular part of the background. Keep the finger and your head in the same place, and close your right eye. Now look at the finger with your left eye and you will see that the finger has shifted position against the background.

The amount of shift depends on how far away the finger is from your eyes. (Try it and see for yourself.) The farther away the finger is from your eyes, the smaller the shift, or parallax. For something very far away from your eyes, you cannot see any shift at all.

To see the parallax of something very far away you have to look at it first from one place, then from another place a distance away.

If something is as far away as a planet or a star, even a mile change in position might not be enough. But what about a change in position of a few hundred miles? You might then see a small shift in the position of a star against the background of other stars. From the amount of the parallax and from the distance between the two viewing places, the distance to a planet or a star can be calculated.

The trouble was that if even the closest stars were very far away, the parallax would be so small it would be very difficult to measure.

In 1838, a German astronomer, Friedrich W. Bessel (BES-ul, 1784–1846), was finally able to detect and measure the small parallax of a nearby star. From that he calculated its distance. Other astronomers quickly reported similar results for other close stars. It turned out that even the nearest stars were not just a billion miles away as Pluto is. They are *thousands* of billions of miles away.

The closest star, we now know, is Proxima Centauri (PROX-ce-ma sen-TAW-ree), and it is 25,000,000-000,000 (twenty-five thousand billion) miles away.

That is just the *nearest* star. There are other stars

FRIEDRICH W. BESSEL

that are much farther away from us than Proxima Centauri is.

It gets complicated talking about the distance of stars in thousands of billions of miles. All those zeroes get confusing. Astronomers have worked out a better way, one that involves light.

Light travels faster than anything else we know. When you turn on a flashlight the beam of light travels outward at a speed of 186,282 miles each second. It would take only 1¼ seconds for a beam of light to travel from the Earth to the Moon. It takes only 8 minutes for a beam of light from the Sun to travel to the Earth over the distance of 93,000,000 miles that separates the two bodies.

How far would a beam of light travel in a year?

There are 31,557,000 seconds in one year. If we multiply that number by 186,282, the number of miles light travels in each one of those seconds, that gives us 5,880,000,000,000 miles. That is almost six thousand billion miles and it is the distance that a beam of light would travel in one year. That distance is called a "light-year."

Proxima Centauri, the nearest star (except for the Sun) is 4.4 light-years away. It takes light 4.4 years to travel the distance from Proxima Centauri to ourselves. When we look at Proxima Centauri, we see it by light that left it 4.4 years ago.

Few people in the United States can see Proxima Centauri, however. It is always so far south in the sky that it can't be seen from farther north than southern Florida.

One star that can be seen in the northern sky is

Sirius (SIR-ee-us), which is the brightest star in the sky at night. It is 8.63 light-years away, and even so, it is one of the nearest stars. The bright star Arcturus (ahrk-TOO-rus) is 40 light-years away.

Astronomers managed to work out the distance of stars that are farther and farther away from us.

One of the bright stars in the constellation of Orion (oh-RYE-on) is called Rigel (RYE-jel). It is 540 light-years away, over 120 times as far away as Proxima Centauri. And, of course, there are stars much farther away with parallaxes so small they can't possibly be measured.

By 1850, it was clear that the universe is *enormous*.

2 The Galaxy

How ENORMOUS MIGHT the universe be? Could it be that the stars spread out over space farther and farther away from us without any end whatever? In that case, the universe would be "infinite" (IN-fih-nit), from Latin words meaning "without end."

Some astronomers suspected this might *not* be so, because of the Milky Way, that band of dim, foggy light that Galileo had found to be composed of very many very faint stars.

In the direction of the Milky Way, there are so many stars so far away that they all blend together into a dim fog. In other directions, there is no such dim fog, which meant to the early astronomers that there could not be vast numbers of stars in those directions. They seemed to come to an end before very great distances were reached.

A German-English astronomer, William Herschel

SPIRAL GALAXY LIKE OUR MILKY WAY

(HER-shel, 1738–1822), considered this matter in 1784, long before the actual distances of the nearest stars were worked out.

He decided to count the stars to see if there were more in some parts of the sky than in others.

Naturally, he couldn't count *all* the stars in the entire sky. There were many millions of stars that could be seen through a telescope, and trying to count them all would be too enormous a job. Instead, Herschel took a shortcut. He selected small patches scattered evenly all over the sky and all of the same size. There were 683 of them, and he counted just the stars in those small patches.

He found that the closer a patch was to the Milky Way, the more stars he could count in it. The smallest number of stars were in the patches that were as far away from the Milky Way as possible.

Could it be that the stars were crowded closer together as one approached the Milky Way?

Herschel didn't think so. He thought it was more sensible to suppose that stars were spread through space evenly, but that in some directions they were spread out for longer distances than in others.

In other words, Herschel didn't think that the stars

HERSCHEL'S 40-FOOT TELESCOPE

were spread out in the shape of a sphere, like a basketball. Suppose they were, and we were at the center—inside the basketball, so to speak. In every direction we looked, we would see to the edge of the spherical ball of stars. It would always be the same distance in whatever direction we looked, however, and we would always see the same number of stars.

Suppose, though, that the stars were spread out in shape like a flattened hamburger patty, and we were in the center. If we looked outward in the direction in which the patty was wide, we would have to look a long, long distance to see to the edge of the collection of stars.

All those many, many stars would fade into a dim fog of light. If the patty were circular, we would see that

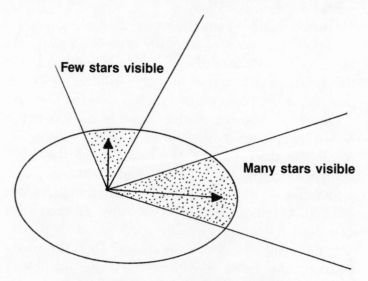

Few stars visible

Many stars visible

**COLLECTION OF STARS WITH THE
SHAPE OF A HAMBURGER PATTY**

fog make a circle about the sky, and that is exactly what the Milky Way does.

If we looked in the direction in which the patty had been flattened and made thin, we would come to the end of the collection of stars pretty soon, and there would be few stars and no fog of light.

If the collection of all the stars we see in the sky had the shape of a patty, then the stars would be strewn more thickly in the sky as one got closer to the luminous band of the Milky Way, just as Herschel had found.

Herschel therefore concluded that the collection of stars which made up the universe had the shape that we see in a hamburger patty. This collection came to be called "the galaxy" (GAL-ak-see), from a Greek word for the Milky Way.

Herschel didn't know how large the galaxy was, for he didn't know how far away any of the stars were. He made some estimates, though, as to how much larger the galaxy was than the average distance (whatever that might be) between two stars.

Once the distance of the nearer stars was determined, people went over Herschel's figures again. According to those figures, the galaxy would be 8,000 light-years across the long way and 1,500 light-years across the short way, and it would contain about 300,000,000 stars. (That is 50,000 times as many stars as we can see without a telescope.)

Is that really the size of the galaxy? Does the galaxy make up the entire universe? If so, the universe is large, but it certainly isn't infinite.

Our solar system

Globular clusters

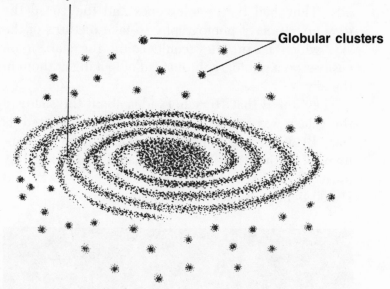

TOP VIEW OF THE MILKY WAY

Our solar system

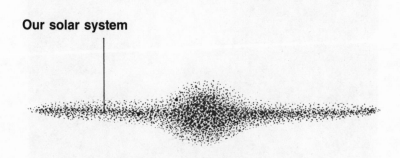

SIDE VIEW OF THE MILKY WAY

Later astronomers improved on Herschel's methods. They had better telescopes and they used the new invention of photography to take pictures of the sky, which meant they could count the stars more easily—on a photograph, instead of looking at them in the sky.

They found that Herschel's idea about the shape of the galaxy was correct but that he underestimated its size. By 1920, a Dutch astronomer, Jacobus C. Kapteyn (KAP-tin, 1851–1922), calculated that the galaxy must be 55,000 light-years across the long way and 11,000 light-years across the short way.

GLOBULAR STAR CLUSTER

Both Herschel and Kapteyn felt that our solar system must be very near the center of the galaxy because the Milky Way looked about equally bright in all directions. But there was one thing about the galaxy which made it seem that the solar system was not in the center. It involved "globular clusters"—thousands of stars crowded into clusters that had a spherical shape.

Herschel himself had discovered them. Altogether about a hundred such clusters were located in the galaxy during the 1800s.

There seemed no reason why the globular clusters shouldn't be spread all through the galaxy. If our solar system was in the center of the galaxy, we ought to see the globular clusters in every direction.

But we don't! Almost every one of those clusters is crowded into half the sky. In fact, one third of them are in the constellation of Sagittarius (SAJ-ih-TAR-ee-us), which takes up only 2 percent of the sky. Why this should be so was a mystery.

Then, in 1912, an American astronomer, Henrietta Swan Leavitt (LEV-it, 1868–1921), was studying certain stars called "Cepheids" (SEE-fee-idz). These are "variable stars" which grow brighter and dimmer in a regular way. Each Cepheid has a certain "period"—that is, a certain time it takes to go through one brightening and one dimming.

Leavitt noticed that the brighter the Cepheid was, the longer its period. This made it possible to work out the distance of objects in the galaxy that were too far to have parallaxes that could be measured.

Suppose, for instance, that an astronomer notices

HARLOW SHAPLEY

two Cepheids, each with the same period. That would mean that the two Cepheids would be equally bright if he were viewing each from the same distance. However, one of those Cepheids appears to be much brighter than the other to his eyes. That can only be because the brighter Cepheid is much closer to him than the dimmer one is. (In the same way, if you see two streetlights and find that one appears brighter than the other, you assume the brighter streetlight is closer.)

It isn't quite that simple, of course, and astronomers had to make many complicated calculations and measurements. Finally, however, they found they could use the Cepheids to measure great distances.

An American astronomer, Harlow Shapley (SHAP-lee, 1885–1972), was particularly interested in doing this. He studied globular clusters very closely and found Cepheids in each one. He measured their periods and their apparent brightness and in this way found just how far away the globular clusters were.

The globular clusters were all *tens of thousands of light-years away*. What's more, from their distance and their position in the sky, they seemed to be arranged in a kind of sphere around a center.

Shapley decided that this center about which the globular clusters were arranged was the center of the galaxy. If so, the center of the galaxy was very far away from us, in the direction of the constellation Sagittarius. That meant the solar system was not at or near the center of the galaxy. It was far toward one of the edges of the galaxy.

In that case, why did the Milky Way seem equally

INTERSTELLAR DUST CLOUD OBSCURING GALAXY

bright all around the sky? Why wasn't the part of the
Milky Way near the constellation Sagittarius, much
brighter than the part in the opposite side of the sky?
(Actually, the Milky Way is a *little* brighter in Sagittarius than anywhere else.)

The reason is that there are clouds of dust and gas
here and there between the stars. Once the telescope
was invented, such clouds could be seen. There are
many such clouds in the Milky Way, and they hide the
stars that lay beyond them and obscure their light.
The light from the center of the galaxy cannot reach us

and we cannot see it. We are near the center of that part of the galaxy that we *can* see.

Shapley hadn't quite allowed for the effect of these clouds, but a Swiss-American astronomer, Robert J. Trumpler (1886–1956), did. He showed how they made the light of the distant stars dimmer than they ought to be from their distance alone. He was able to show that the galaxy was 100,000 light-years across the long way, and about 16,000 light-years across the short way, at its center.

Our solar system is about 30,000 light-years from the center and 20,000 light-years from the near edge. The galaxy is thickest at the center and gets thinner toward the edge. In the place where our solar system is, the galaxy is only 3,000 light-years thick.

Thus the galaxy is much larger than Kapteyn had thought, in the time before the Cepheids had been used to measure distances. The galaxy is now known to contain up to, perhaps, 300,000,000,000 (three hundred billion) stars. About 80 percent of these stars are considerably smaller than our Sun, however. If all the stars in the galaxy were the same size as our Sun, there would be about 100,000,000,000 of them.

3 The Other Galaxies

FOR NEARLY A hundred fifty years after Herschel had first worked out the shape of the galaxy, astronomers seemed to think that the galaxy was all there was. They might argue about just how large the galaxy might be, but whatever its size, it appeared to be the whole universe. At least so it seemed. The telescopes didn't show the astronomers anything that seemed to lie outside the galaxy.

There was one exception. Deep in the southern sky there are two foggy patches of light that look as though they are pieces of the Milky Way that broke loose. They are called the "Magellanic Clouds" (MAJ-uh-LAN-ik), in honor of Portuguese navigator Ferdinand Magellan (muh-JEL-an, 1480–1522).

When Magellan led his ships on the very first voyage around the world, the lookout on his ship was the first European ever to see the Magellanic Clouds. This was at a time when the ship was near the southern tip of South America, for the two clouds are so far south that they are never seen from northern nations, such as those of Europe.

If the Magellanic Clouds are studied through a telescope, they can be seen to be composed of large numbers of very faint stars, just as the Milky Way is. Some of those stars are Cepheids. In fact, it was the Cepheids in the Magellanic Clouds that Leavitt was studying when she found that the brighter ones had longer periods.

From the periods of these Cepheids, astronomers were able to show that of the two clouds, the larger

LARGE MAGELLANIC CLOUD

one was 155,000 light-years away and the smaller one was 165,000 light-years away.

The clouds are well outside our galaxy, and they could be looked at as separate galaxies that are much smaller than ours. The larger cloud may contain as many as 10,000,000,000 (ten billion) stars and the smaller one perhaps only 2,000,000,000 (two billion) stars. Both clouds, put together, have perhaps only one twentieth as many stars as our galaxy has.

It could be, then, that the whole universe is made up of our galaxy, plus two small satellite galaxies, and that's all.

However, there was one object that was puzzling. In 1612, a German astronomer, Simon Marius (1570–1624), had described a small patch of dim light in the constellation Andromeda (an-DROM-uh-duh). It was a "nebula" (NEB-yoo-luh), from a Latin word for "cloud." Because of its location, it was called the "Andromeda nebula."

Most astronomers thought that it was a cloud of dust and gas. Such nebulas sometimes glowed because there were stars inside the cloud. In fact, some astronomers thought the Andromeda nebula was a cloud of dust and gas that was settling together under the pull of its own gravity, and that it was just forming the star that gave it light.

In 1799, a French astronomer, Pierre de Laplace (lah-PLAHS, 1749–1827), suggested that our own solar system had formed out of such a huge cloud of swirling gas. This was called the "nebular hypothesis" (hy-POTH-uh-sis), after the Andromeda nebula.

There was a catch. Other nebulas, which had stars

ANDROMEDA GALAXY

lighting the gas and dust of which they were formed, emitted light that contained only a few wavelengths of light. (Light is made up of very tiny waves of different lengths.) The Andromeda nebula, however, emitted light of every possible wavelength, just as stars did. The light from the Andromeda nebula was not like that of clouds of dust and gas lit by stars but seemed like *starlight* itself. Could it actually be made up of stars?

The trouble with this idea was that no stars could be seen in the Andromeda nebula. It appeared to be just an even fog of dim white light.

Every once in a while, though, tiny points of light could be seen in the Andromeda nebula, like very dim stars that only lasted a short while and faded away.

There are indeed such things as temporarily bright stars. Sometimes stars suddenly brighten considerably, then fade away to their original dimness. If the star is too dim to be seen ordinarily, it might become visible while it is in its bright stage, then fade away to invisibility again. In the days before the telescope such stars, which seemed to appear and disappear, were called *novae stellae*, which is Latin for "new stars." Today they are called "novas," for short.

Could the occasional points of light in the Andromeda nebula be connected with the nebula? Or could they just be appearing in the galaxy somewhere in the space in front of the nebula but have no connection at all with that little patch of luminous fog?

An American astronomer, Heber D. Curtis (1872–1942), studied the problem in the early 1900s. If the novas were just appearing in the space in front of the nebula, then they should be appearing in the same way in other directions, too—at least in some other directions.

But they weren't. A great many novas appeared in the Andromeda nebula (by now, about a hundred have been detected), but nowhere else in the sky do so many appear in such a small area. It couldn't just be that the space in front of the Andromeda nebula was so unusual. It had to be that the novas were appearing *inside* the nebula and that it was the nebula that was unusual.

Another point about the novas in the Andromeda nebula was that they were very dim. They were much dimmer than the novas that appeared in other places in the sky. Could it be that the Andromeda novas were very dim because they were very far away—much farther away than anything else in the galaxy? If so, it might be that the Andromeda nebula was composed of stars, but that those stars could not be seen because the nebula was so far away that individual stars simply could not be made out.

In 1885, a star had appeared in the Andromeda nebula, one that was a nova, but *much* brighter than any of the other novas. It was so bright that it could almost be seen without a telescope. Could *it* have been part of the nebula?

It turned out that there were some very few novas that appeared in other parts of the sky that were *much* brighter than ordinary novas there. One such star appeared in the sky in 1572 and, for a time, was brighter than the planet Venus, then faded away. The Swiss astronomer Fritz Zwicky (1898–1974) called such unusually bright novas, "supernovas."

Before outburst

At maximum

After maximum

NOVA OF 1925

A supernova could, for just a short time, be 100,000,000,000 (a hundred billion) times as bright as an ordinary star. What if the star of 1885 was a supernova that had appeared in the Andromeda nebula? It would be as bright as the entire nebula for a short period of time and it was.

But then, why should that supernova of the Andromeda nebula have been so dim that it couldn't be seen without a telescope, when the supernova of 1572 was brighter than Venus? Curtis decided that the supernova of 1572 must have been rather close to us, while the supernova of 1885 was in the Andromeda nebula, which was *very* far away.

For some years there was considerable dispute among astronomers as to whether the Andromeda nebula was inside our galaxy, or was far beyond it.

Then, in 1917, a new telescope was put into use, in California. It had a mirror that was one hundred inches across and it was the largest and best telescope that had been built up to that time. Using it was an American astronomer, Edwin P. Hubble (1889–1953), and he was able to take photographs which finally showed that the Andromeda nebula was made up of vast crowds of very tiny stars.

Curtis was right. The Andromeda nebula had to be very far away.

It really was another galaxy, even larger than our own. From that point on, it came to be called the "Andromeda galaxy." Eventually, Cepheids were made out in the Andromeda galaxy and from their periods and apparent brightness, the distance of the new galaxy could be calculated.

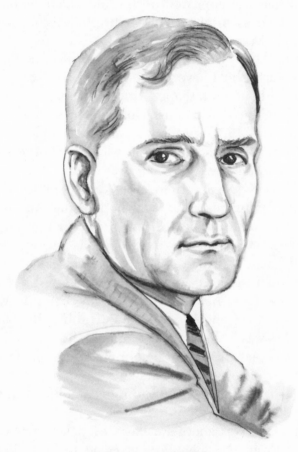

EDWIN P. HUBBLE

At first the calculation came out too low, but in 1952, a German-American astronomer, Walter Baade (BAH-duh, 1893–1960), showed that there were two kinds of Cepheids. That changed the method of calculation. When it was done correctly, it turned out that the Andromeda galaxy was 2,300,000 light-years away. It was fifteen times as far away as the Magellanic Clouds, and it contained about twice as many stars as our own galaxy does.

Once it was understood that the Andromeda nebula was a galaxy, many other galaxies were found. Our own galaxy turned out to be only one of very many, and sometimes it is called the Milky Way galaxy to distinguish it from the rest.

The Milky Way galaxy, the Andromeda galaxy, the Magellanic Clouds (which are now considered to be two "dwarf galaxies"), and about two dozen other dwarf galaxies make up a *cluster* of galaxies that are called the "local group."

Altogether, astronomers have detected millions of galaxies, almost all of which are divided into clusters. Some of the clusters are huge and contain thousands of galaxies. The farthest galaxies we can see are hundreds of millions of light-years away. That means that the light by which we see such very distant galaxies started on its long journey to us hundreds of millions of years ago, when the only life on Earth consisted of simple microscopic creatures.

In 1963, astronomers discovered "quasars" (KWAY-zarz). Some scientists think they are very distant galaxies with very bright centers. They are so far away that only the very bright centers can be seen. For this reason, the quasars look like dim stars. However, they are *billions* of light-years away. The farthest quasar we know is more than 10,000,000,000 (ten billion) light-years away. The light it emits started on its journey to us billions of years before the Earth came into existence.

Counting the very distant galaxies we can't see, there may be as many as 100,000,000,000 (a hundred billion) galaxies altogether, and the universe may be as much as 25,000,000,000 (twenty-five billion) light-years across. Our own galaxy is as a tiny dust grain compared to the whole universe.

4 The Receding Galaxies

DID THE UNIVERSE always exist? Will it always continue to exist? The answers to such questions depend upon certain discoveries about light.

When sunlight, which is a mixture of tiny waves of all sorts of wavelengths, is passed through a triangle of glass called a "prism" (PRIZ-um), the rays of light bend. The longer wavelengths bend less than the shorter wavelengths. Therefore a band of light is produced in which all the wavelengths are lined up in order, the longest wavelengths at one end, the shortest at the other. This is called a "spectrum" (SPEK-trum).

Different wavelengths seem to have different colors to our eyes, so the spectrum is a rainbow of color. Red is at the long-wavelength end, then orange, yellow, green, blue, and, finally, violet is at the short-wavelength end.

Some wavelengths happen to be missing in sunlight. As a result, there are places in the spectrum where there is no light. A dark line crosses the spectrum and is called a "spectral line." There are thousands of such lines in the spectrum of sunlight.

Spectra can be obtained from other sources of light, and these may have different patterns of spectral lines.

When a source of light is coming toward us, all the

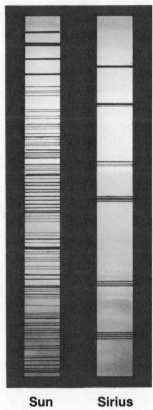

Sun   Sirius

SPECTRA OF THE SUN AND SIRIUS

wavelengths of the light we receive are shortened. The spectral lines are therefore shifted toward the violet end of the spectrum. This is a "violet shift." When a source of light is going away from us, all the wavelengths of the light we receive are lengthened. The spectral lines are shifted toward the red end of the spectrum, and this is a "red shift."

This shifting of lines is called a "Doppler-Fizeau effect." It was first explained, in 1842, by an Austrian scientist, Christian J. Doppler (DOP-ler, 1803–53). He worked it out in connection with sound, but soon afterward, a French scientist, Armand H. L. Fizeau (fee-ZOH, 1819–96), showed that it worked for light also.

This should tell us something about stars. Starlight can be spread into a spectrum with dark lines crossing it. Astronomers learned to recognize particular dark

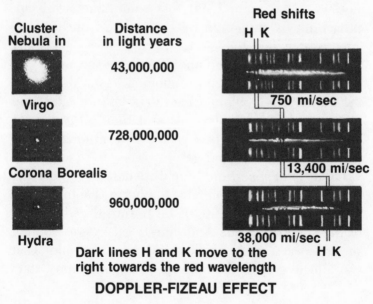

Cluster Nebula in	Distance in light years	Red shifts H K
Virgo	43,000,000	750 mi/sec
Corona Borealis	728,000,000	13,400 mi/sec
Hydra	960,000,000	38,000 mi/sec

Dark lines H and K move to the right towards the red wavelength   H K

DOPPLER-FIZEAU EFFECT

lines and to know exactly where each is supposed to be in the spectrum. If the actual position is shifted a little toward the violet, then the star is approaching us; if it is shifted a little toward the red, the star is receding from us. From the amount of the shift, the speed of approach or recession can be calculated.

In 1868, a British astronomer, William Huggins (1824–1910), was finally able to form the very faint spectrum of the star Sirius. He noticed a tiny shift of the lines toward the red and he could tell that Sirius was moving away from us. The best present-day observations tell us that it is receding from us at a speed of about 5 miles a second.

Afterward, various astronomers obtained the spectra of other stars and found out how fast they were moving, either toward us or away from us. They were not surprised to find out that some stars were approaching us and some were receding from us. The speeds at which they were moving were mostly between 5 miles a second and 70 miles a second.

In 1912, an American astronomer, Vesto M. Slipher (SLY-fer, 1875–1969), managed to obtain the spectrum of the Andromeda galaxy. At that time, of course, it was not yet known to be a galaxy. It was thought to be just a cloud of dust and gas.

On its faint spectrum there were dark lines, just like those in starlight or sunlight. Slipher was able to show that the lines were shifted a bit toward the violet end of the spectrum. The Andromeda galaxy was coming toward us at a speed of about 120 miles a second. That was a little greater than the speed at which most stars

VESTO M. SLIPHER

moved, but some stars did move that quickly, so Slipher wasn't troubled by the figure.

He went on to study the spectra of other nebulas that showed dark lines, and by 1917 he had worked with fifteen of them.

By that time he had two problems. He would have expected that about half of the nebulas would be approaching and half would be receding, but that's not how it was. The Andromeda nebula and one other were approaching. The remaining thirteen were *all receding.*

The second problem was the speed of recession. The average speed for the thirteen receding nebulas was about 400 miles per second. This was a much higher speed than that at which any known star moved.

As Slipher made more measurements, he continued to find only recessions, and the speeds continued to get higher and higher. When Hubble showed that these nebula were really distant galaxies, astronomers began to wonder all the more why the galaxies moved so quickly when nothing else moved as quickly, and why they all receded. The two galaxies that were approaching were part of the local group. Every single galaxy outside the local group was receding, without exception.

Working for Hubble was another astronomer, Milton L. Humason (HYOO-muh-son, 1891–1972), who continued to work with the spectra of distant galaxies. He exposed the light from these very dim galaxies to a camera night after night in order to build up the light to the point where he had a photograph he

MILTON L. HUMASON

could study. In 1928, he obtained the spectrum of a faint galaxy that was receding at a speed of 2,400 miles a second. In 1936, he managed to get the spectrum of a galaxy that was receding at a speed of 25,000 miles a second.

Such speeds seemed very strange indeed. How could they be explained?

Hubble was particularly interested. He did his very best to estimate how far away all these distant galaxies were. He used all sorts of ways to make an estimate and he ended up by placing in order of increasing distance all the galaxies whose spectra had been studied.

When he did this, he discovered something unusual. The farther away a galaxy was, the more quickly it was receding. In fact, the speed of recession increased by a fixed amount for every additional bit of distance. This is called "Hubble's Law," and it was first advanced in 1929.

But why should this be so? Why should all the galaxies (except a couple in our local group) be receding from us? And why should they be receding from us more and more quickly, the more and more distant they are from us?

The answer came as a result of the work that had been done by a German-born scientist, Albert Einstein (INE-stine, 1879–1955). In 1915, he had worked out a new kind of description of the universe based on what was called "the General Theory of Relativity." As part of that theory, Einstein worked out a set of "field equations" that described what the properties of the universe as a whole would have to be.

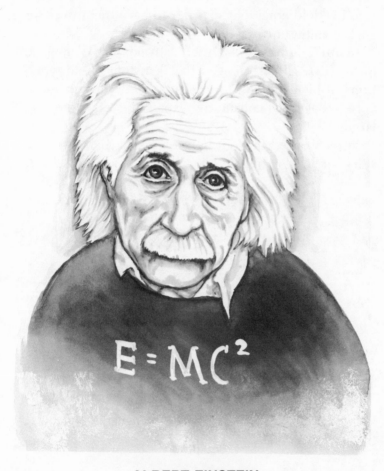

ALBERT EINSTEIN

Einstein himself thought the universe should be considered "static"—that is, it didn't change with time. For that reason, he introduced another figure into his field equations in order to have them work for such a static universe.

In 1917, however, a Dutch astronomer, Willem de Sitter (1872–1934), showed that Einstein's field equations, if his new figure were left out, described a universe that was constantly expanding and growing larger.

Sitter worked this out by pretending there were no stars or other objects in the universe. In 1922,

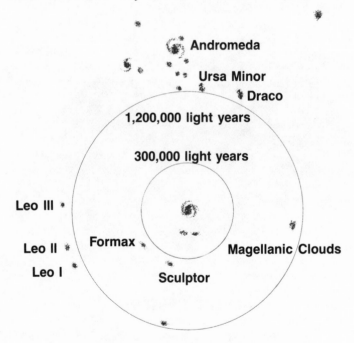

THE LOCAL GROUP OF GALAXIES

however, a Russian mathematician, Alexander A. Friedman (1888–1925), showed that the field equations meant an expanding universe, even if the stars were taken into account. In 1930, an English astronomer, Arthur S. Eddington (1882–1944), showed that even if Einstein's static universe existed, it wouldn't stay static. It would start either to expand or to contract, and either way it would continue to do so.

Einstein had to leave the field equations the way he had them in the first place. He said afterward that inventing that figure was the worst mistake he had ever made.

Einstein's field equations explained Hubble's Law. The universe was expanding. Clusters of galaxies were held together by gravitational pull, but different clusters kept moving apart because the universe, as it expanded, pulled them apart.

If you suppose that every part of the universe is expanding at the same rate, then we would indeed observe exactly what Hubble observed. All the galaxies outside the local group would be receding from us. The farther away they were, the faster they would seem to be receding.

This wouldn't make us special. If we were watching the sky from any other galaxy, we would see the same thing. It isn't that the clusters of galaxies are receding from us particularly; *they are all receding from each other*.

This notion of the expanding universe, based on Einstein's theory and Hubble's Law, brings us face to face with the questions of the beginning and the end of the universe.

5 The Big Bang

Suppose we think about the expanding universe for a while. Since it is expanding, it is bigger this year than it was last year—and it was bigger last year than it was the year before—and bigger the year before than it was the year before that—and so on.

In fact, if we look *back* in time, it would seem that the universe would get smaller and smaller and smaller until it shrank down to nothing.

The first person to speak out about this was a Belgian astronomer, Georges E. Lemaitre (luh-MET-ruh, 1894–1966). In 1927, he said that at some long past time everything in the universe was squashed together into a very small object he called the "cosmic egg."

He thought that this cosmic egg suddenly exploded and flew apart and that the universe is still expanding as part of this original explosion.

This view was taken up and supported by a Russian-

American scientist, George Gamow (1904–68). He called this explosion of the cosmic egg the "Big Bang," and he considered it the beginning of the universe.

How far back in time would we have to go to imagine the universe shrunk to a very compact size? When did the Big Bang take place, and how old is the universe now?

That depends on how fast the universe is expanding.

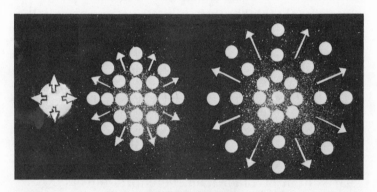

THE BIG BANG

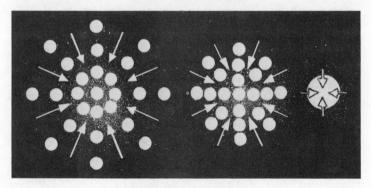

THE BIG CRUNCH

The faster it is expanding, the faster it has grown in the past, and the less time it took for the universe to expand to its present size.

Back in 1929, Hubble had worked out how fast the universe was expanding, and the rate depended on a figure he had worked out called the "Hubble constant." The larger the Hubble constant, the faster the universe had expanded, and the shorter the time since the Big Bang. The original figure for the Hubble constant made it look as though the Big Bang had taken place 2,000,000,000 (two billion) years ago and that the universe was therefore that old.

This figure came as a terrible surprise to scientists who studied the Earth. (Such scientists are "geologists" [jee-OL-uh-jists].) There were rocks on Earth that they were sure were over three billion years old, and they were quite certain that the solar system had formed out of a cloud of dust and gas about 4,600,000,000 (4.6 billion) years ago. How could the solar system be older than the entire universe?

For over 20 years, this puzzle was not solved. Who were right, the astronomers or the geologists?

Then, in 1952, when Baade showed there were two kinds of Cepheids, it turned out that the astronomers had been wrong. By making use of the Cepheids to measure distance in a new way, it turned out that the universe was much larger than they had thought earlier. That meant the value of the Hubble constant was considerably smaller than had been thought. And that meant it had taken longer for the universe to expand to the size it now was, so that the Big Bang was much longer ago than had been thought.

The universe is certainly older than the solar system, but how much older is not certain. Some astronomers think the Big Bang took place as recently as 10,000,000,000 (ten billion) years ago, and some think it took place as long as 20,000,000,000 (twenty billion) years ago. It might be best to take an average and say that the universe may be 15,000,000,000 (fifteen billion) years old.

Some astronomers were not certain the Big Bang had taken place at all. They thought that even though the galaxies were moving apart and the universe was expanding, new matter might be slowly forming and new young galaxies would be appearing in the spaces left by the old galaxies as they pulled apart.

This was the theory of "continuous creation," and it was advanced in 1948 by an English astronomer, Fred Hoyle (1915–   ), and by two Austrian-born astronomers, Hermann Bondi (1919–   ) and Thomas Gold (1920–   ). If continuous creation was correct, the universe looked just about the same as far back in time as we can go. The universe could be considered as having lasted forever and as having no beginning.

At about the time that continuous creation had been suggested, however, Gamow had pointed out that if there were a Big Bang, it must have filled the universe (which was very tiny at first) with radiation that was very hot—trillions of trillions of degrees. As the universe expanded, however, the radiation expanded, too, and its temperature dropped rapidly.

By now, billions of years after the Big Bang, the average temperature of the universe must have cooled down to a very low temperature indeed. What's more, radiation is very short-wave when it is hot, and the waves grow longer as the temperature gets lower. By now the radiation of the original Big Bang must have stretched out its wavelengths till they are in the form of what we call "radio waves."

Gamow thought, therefore, that if there were some way of detecting them, a faint background of radio waves should be found in the sky. The farther one looked into space with telescopes, the longer it took radiation to reach us from the greater and greater distances that were reached. If one looked far enough into space, radiation would reach us that had been traveling ever since the Big Bang. In no matter what direction we looked, if we looked far enough, we would reach evidence of the Big Bang. The radio waves should come from every direction, therefore, in exactly the same way. They would be a kind of faint whisper reaching us from that huge explosion in the past.

At the time Gamow suggested this, there were no instruments capable of picking up faint radio-wave signals from the sky, but as the years passed, astronomers built better and better "radio telescopes." In 1964, an American astronomer, Robert H. Dicke (DIK-ee, 1916–   ), revived Gamow's notion.

The search for the background radio-wave radiation began at once. In 1965, two American astronomers, Arno A. Penzias (PEN-zee-us, 1933–   ) and Robert W. Wilson (1936–   ), set up very delicate systems for detecting such radiation. Soon they were able to report having detected the radiation and found it to be exactly as Gamow had felt it ought to be.

Since then, many astronomers have studied the background radiation, and it is considered strong evidence that the Big Bang *did* take place. The possibility of continuous creation has faded out.

In fact, as we look into the distance with our telescopes, the farthest quasar we see is over 10,000,000,000 (ten billion) light-years away. The light we see it by must have left it ten billion years ago, not

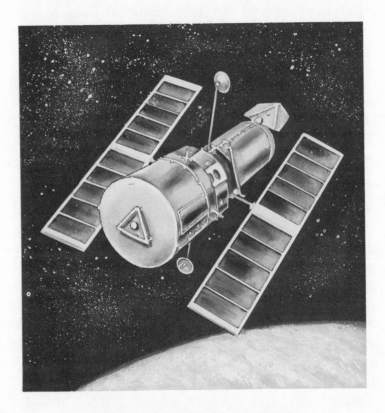

SPACE TELESCOPE IN ORBIT

long after the Big Bang. Can we detect quasars that are farther away still? Perhaps not. There seems to be a haze beyond the farthest quasars and we may be looking into the hot radiation of the Big Bang, perhaps twelve or fifteen billion years ago.

And what is going to happen in the future?

One possibility is that the universe will simply continue to expand—and expand—and expand forever. The galaxies will continue to recede until, trillions of years from now, all of them, except for those in the local group, will be too far away to see using any instruments. This is an "open universe."

However, the galaxies, as they move apart, are always being pulled upon by each other's gravitational force. The gravitation causes the expansion to slow down with time. It may be that, eventually, the expansion will slow down to zero. The universe may stop expanding, and then, very slowly, start to contract. The contraction would continue, faster and faster, until all the galaxies will come together in a "Big Crunch." This would be a "closed universe."

If the universe is closed, it may be that the material for the Big Bang came out of nothing and that with the Big Crunch it will go back into nothing. Or else, when the Big Crunch comes, the galaxies will crush together only so far and then will "bounce" in a new Big Bang. It may be that the universe expands and contracts, then expands and contracts, then expands and contracts and so on forever. This would be an "oscillating universe."

Well, is the universe open or closed? If it is closed, is it a one-time universe, or an oscillating universe?

Astronomers are not entirely certain. Whether the universe will continue to expand forever, or whether it will someday stop expanding and begin to contract depends on how strong the universe's gravitational pull is. The strength of that pull depends on how much matter exists in the volume of the universe. It depends on how many galaxies and stars and other "mass," giving rise to gravitational pull, are squeezed into the volume of the universe.

If we consider the stars and galaxies alone, then there seems to be only one one-hundredth as much mass in the volume of the universe as is needed to stop the expansion. If that is so, then the universe is open.

Some astronomers think, though, that there may be some mass that we're leaving out of consideration. (This is called "the problem of the missing mass.") Maybe there is mass outside the galaxies. Maybe there are tiny particles that we think have no mass but that actually *do* have mass.

In that case, it may be that we'll eventually decide the universe is closed. And we may discover ways of deciding whether a closed universe will oscillate or not.

There's still a great deal to find out about the universe, but then, think how dull it would be for scientists, and for all of us, if all the questions about the universe were answered and there was nothing more to find out.

Index